Frida

by Jonah Winter   illustrated by Ana Juan

Arthur A. Levine Books   An Imprint of Scholastic Press

For my mother.

— J. W.

To the little artist

who is in your heart.

— A. J.

Frida enters the world.

For little Frida, the world is Mexico.

Her house is a blue house. It is in the town of Coyoacán.

Frida's father is an artist
and a photographer.

He teaches her how to use
a paintbrush.

Frida's mother takes care
of six daughters.
Often, she is tired.

Often, Frida is lonely,
even though she has sisters.

Enter, stage left: Frida's imaginary friend. Her name is also Frida.

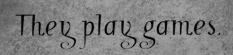

They play games.

All of a sudden, Frida falls very ill. She's in bed for months. There's something wrong with one of her legs. Even her imaginary friend can't cheer her.

That's when Frida teaches herself how to draw. Drawing saves her from being sad.

After Frida gets well,
she still wants to make
art. So she paints little
paintings. They are
copies of other paintings.

Painting onto photographs is what Frida's father does for a living. He teaches her how to do this too.

Frida also paints things she sees through a microscope.
She loves looking at things very closely.

At school, Frida studies science.

She is bored. School is too easy.

One day Frida is riding the bus home from school.

A horrible accident happens.

A trolley runs into the bus.
Frida almost dies.

In the hospital, it is painting that
saves her once again.
Painting is like her imaginary friend.
It is there whenever she wants it.
It keeps her company.
It keeps her from giving up hope.

After the accident, life will never be the same for Frida.
She will walk with a cane—when she is able to walk.
Her body will hurt, always.

But Frida doesn't cry or complain. Instead of crying, she paints pictures of herself crying.

When she can't leave her bed, she paints in bed.

When her whole torso is put in a cast, she paints on the cast.

Nothing can stop Frida from painting.
Because she's so often alone, unable to
leave her house, she has to use
her imagination.

She paints what she sees in her heart—
on top of what she sees with her eyes.
It's almost like painting on photographs.

She paints little magical
scenes with words at the bottom.
All over Mexico, people paint these
kinds of scenes. Sometimes they are
scenes of accidents with angels coming
to the rescue. They are like prayers
for people who are sick. They
are called *exvotos*. Frida
paints *exvotos* of
herself when she is
sick or in pain.

Frida imitates
no one in her style. Her
paintings are like nothing
else. In museums, people still
look at them and weep and
sigh and smile. She turns
her pain into something
beautiful. It is like a
miracle.

AUTHOR'S NOTE

FRIDA KAHLO WAS BORN ON JULY 6, 1907, in Coyoacán, Mexico, to Guillermo Kahlo and Matilde Calderón de Kahlo. At the age of seven, she was stricken with polio, confined to bed for nine months, and left with a shrunken right leg and a limp. At the age of eighteen, she was in a horrible bus accident that is too nightmarish to describe here.

It's a miracle that she survived and that she was able to produce any art, considering the constant pain she was in throughout the rest of her life. That her paintings are among the most beautiful and original art ever created is a monument to Kahlo's indomitable spirit and willpower. That her paintings continue to be exhibited in museums all over the world and are reproduced in books, on posters, and even in advertisements is proof of her lasting popularity.

Kahlo's popularity, which has been increasing steadily over the years since her death on July 13, 1954, began to grow when she married the world-renowned Mexican muralist Diego Rivera in 1929. Their personalities were both so colorful, and their love for each other so intense, that their marriage remains one of the most famous of the twentieth century.

But it wasn't merely Kahlo's association with the celebrated Rivera that sparked an ongoing public fascination with her. Her painful story is so inspirational that she has become a role model for artists in general, who often must work under difficult conditions. She has specifically been an inspiration to women artists, who have found in Kahlo's strength, courage, and pizzazz an example of how to thrive as a woman in an art world dominated by men.

ARTIST'S NOTE

WORLD-RENOWNED PAINTER FRIDA KAHLO made an important contribution to Mexican art and culture. And in turn, Mexican art and culture played an important part in Frida's development as an artist.

For this reason I have portrayed traditional characters in Mexican folk art—funny skeletons, little devils, sweet jaguars, and others—as constant companions throughout her life. These are images she would have seen in her childhood home, in the markets of her town, and in books. Photographs of the home she shared with Diego Rivera show these characters proudly displayed in the folk art that decorated their rooms.

And as these characters inspired Frida Kahlo, so has Frida Kahlo inspired me. I hope she will inspire you too.

Text copyright © 2002 by Jonah Winter • Illustrations copyright © 2002 by Ana Juan
All rights reserved. Published by Scholastic Press, a division of Scholastic Inc., Publishers since 1920.
SCHOLASTIC, SCHOLASTIC PRESS, and the LANTERN LOGO are trademarks and/or registered trademarks of Scholastic Inc.

LIBRARY OF CONGRESS CATALOGING-IN-PUBLICATION DATA
Winter, Jonah
Frida/by Jonah Winter • illustrated by Ana Juan.   p.   cm.   ISBN 0-590-20320-7
1. Kahlo, Frida—Juvenile literature. 2. Painters—Mexico—Biography—Juvenile literature. I. Kahlo, Frida. II. Juan, Ana.
III. Title. ND259.K33 W56 2002 759.972—dc21 [B] 00-051421

The art was created using acrylics and wax on paper. The text was set in GF Hegemonic. The display type was set in Zaragoza.
Book design by Marijka Kostiw and Ana Juan

10 9 8 7 6 5 4 3   02 03 04 05 06

Printed in Mexico   49 • First edition, February 2002